Confessions of a
Contemplative Crossing Guard

"*Confessions of a Contemplative Crossing Guard* is a heartwarming story by Rabbi Robert Eisen. He recently took on a role as a crossing guard, and through this experience, he paints a vivid picture of his interactions with school staff and the children and families he is charged to keep safe while crossing the street. Rabbi Eisen imparts words of wisdom, shares stories from religious texts and reflective passages that will resonate with readers long after they have finished the book."

—MERYL L. WARDA, child and family therapist

"A cleverly written and relatable book by recalling his journey from rabbi to crossing guard, Bob Eisen has created thoughtful, inspirational, and meaningful stories and questions that cause wonder and deeper insights. This book is for every human being, young or old, and it combines both simplicity and complexity of thought. This book should be a book club favorite as it is provocative and inspires depth and sharing. A must-read."

—ALICE STEINFELD, licensed professional counselor

"In *Confessions of a Contemplative Crossing Guard*, Rabbi Robert Eisen shares with the reader the sometimes surprising and often serious questions and observations that emerge from his mindful moments making sure the neighborhood children get to and from school safely. In a conversational tone, he invites the reader into thoughtful and deeply rooted reflections on some of life's fundamental questions. His clear thinking, always informed by the truths of Torah, and clear vision of the real world provides the reader with an accessible and intelligible way to focus on what matters."

—STEVEN S. MASON, rabbi emeritus,
North Shore Congregation Israel

"In *Confessions of a Contemplative Crossing Guard*, Rabbi Eisen is a humble, humorous observer of human quirks and foibles, yet he provides sound guidance for those who seek to live a well-considered life."

—KATHERINE (SCHOOL PSYCHOLOGIST)
AND AARON LEONARD

Confessions of a
Contemplative Crossing Guard

Reflections on the "Why" of Crossing the Road
and What It Can Mean When We Do

ROBERT J. EISEN

RESOURCE *Publications* · Eugene, Oregon

CONFESSIONS OF A CONTEMPLATIVE CROSSING GUARD
Reflections on the "Why" of Crossing the Road and What It Can Mean
When We Do

Resource Publications
An Imprint of Wipf and Stock Publishers
199 W. 8th Ave., Suite 3
Eugene, OR 97401

www.wipfandstock.com

PAPERBACK ISBN: 979-8-3852-1378-8
HARDCOVER ISBN: 979-8-3852-1379-5
EBOOK ISBN: 979-8-3852-1380-1

VERSION NUMBER 05/17/24

Dedicated to our grandson, Remy,
who is just learning to crawl (and now walk!),
but teaching us so much about how we can and should
be crossing the roads life places before us ourselves

הַנִּסְתָּרֹת לַיֵי אֱלֹהֵינוּ וְהַנִּגְלֹת לָנוּ וּלְבָנֵינוּ עַד־עוֹלָם

The secret things belong to the Lord our God;

but that which is revealed belongs to us

DEUTERONOMY 29:28

Contents

Acknowledgments

FIRST AND FOREMOST, I need to acknowledge the influence two of my former congregants had on me. If not for them, and what they taught me, I would have never noticed much less thought about responding to the ad for a crossing guard. Those congregants were Meryl and Phyllis Broad. Though I was involved with the burial of both, it was how they lived their lives that had the greatest impact (especially on me).

Meryl was already retired when I met him. In his retirement he served as the crossing guard for the elementary school down the street from where he lived, and just down the block from my synagogue. Passing by his corner as I did almost every morning and afternoon, there he would be with a smile on his face. Sitting in a lawn chair until his charges made their way to his crosswalk, he would wave to everyone who passed by. He probably could not always tell who was in the car, but that did not matter to him. Everyone was embraced the same way. When the students arrived, he would enable them to cross with great precision, even carrying the littlest ones when the monsoons had left their mark and the street was flooded. (the street in front of the school had no drainage and would often flood). He received the recognition we knew he deserved when he was named Crossing Guard of the Year for Tucson Unified School District.

Though over the years Phyllis was involved with every aspect of the congregation's educational program, when I arrived in 1999, she was the primary teacher in our conversion program. She was a crossing guard in her own right, enabling her students to make the transition from one side of their lives to an other. Phyllis was the kind of teacher I always wanted to be. She nurtured her students with such love and concern, making each comfortable with who they were and what they were doing. Conversion, after all, is not something that anyone takes lightly. She gave her students the knowledge, experience, and vision of the form and function (history) of Judaism so they could see their own place in our ever-evolving heritage.

And yet, what is most important to note is that in her professional life Phyllis was a social worker. When I first met her, she was working with hospice patients and their families. How much more of a crossing guard could anyone be?

What Meryl and Phyllis taught me over the years is at the foundation of every day I am on the job. Though I am not sure what they would have said about today, when I screamed at two cars that were not stopping even when there were people in the crosswalk and just about threw my stop sign at a third. However, we all made it through the day. I am learning some very interesting dance steps as I simultaneously avoid the cars that do not want to even slow down, much less stop, and watch out for the students.

I owe much to the administration, staff, faculty, students, and families at the school. It is they who enable and inspire me to do what I can in this position. In the scheme of things, the role I play is miniscule compared to the worth of so many others. In fact, I am not even sure they put a substitute in place the few times that I was out. However, they do make the job interesting, and sometimes even fun. I am thankful for the opportunity they have afforded me.

Phyllis Braun offered commentary and insight that gave a much-needed form to the words, sentences, and paragraphs. Katherine and Aaron Leonard, Rabbi Steven Mason, Alice Steinfeld and Meryl Warda each helped me make sense out what I had written in new and different ways.

And, I want to especially thank my son and daughter-in-law, Alex and Carly; our grandchildren, Reese and Remy; and "granddog" Piper, for everything they are to me. My wife, Debby, has been my own personal "crossing guard" for over four decades. If there is anything good that I have accomplished in life, and especially this exercise, it should be attributed to her.

In the meantime, it is 3:00 p.m., it is time to go play in traffic!

Introduction

OUR MOVE TO PHOENIX from Tucson in 2020, coincidental with the lockdown and quarantining that came with the COVID-19 pandemic, left us with few options for "entertainment." We knew the area and were pleased with the neighborhood in which we had settled. However, the closest we got to meeting anyone was through the computer. To find some semblance of order and purpose, I began walking our son's dog, Piper. We would go for long walks almost every morning, exploring their neighborhood. Other walkers would pass by and we were all careful to keep our distance. Even Piper became accustomed to my moving her off to the side or falling back and letting others pass by, except for when we approached the elementary school that was on our route no matter which way we went.

Whenever we walked past the school, Piper would stop and stare or try to cross the street to get a closer sniff. The parking lot was usually pretty empty (school was online) and the building was quiet. However, somehow, she seemed to know that that was not always the case. As the days turned to weeks, and then to months, and then with the new year the isolation started to break up, Piper was drawn to the school even more. The activity, the voices of the children, what we imagined to be the smell of the cafeteria perceptible only to dogs (!), all drew her to want to get closer. But she knew the routine and would look at me, and then proceed on our path.

Sometimes my wife, Debby, joined us on these walks. The three of us would make our way along the different routes as I provided "color commentary" regarding what we were looking at and how Piper had responded the last time we had gone that way. Well, one day, in December of 2022, while the three of us were en route, I had to stop and tie my shoe. Debby took Piper and I bent over to tie my shoe. When I looked up, I noticed the sign in front of the elementary school was advertising for a "PM Crossing Guard." I half-jokingly said something about how that might be interesting and called the school from where we were across the street. The person who answered the phone said they had been advertising the position since August and that no one had applied. It was still open and I was encouraged to apply. When we got home, I logged onto the school's website and filled out the application. My wife, (who was/is a teacher and knows how the system works) laughed at how nervous I was regarding the application process. "Are you kidding me?" she said. "You are the first and only warm body that has applied. You have no competition. You will get the job."

I did!

With a bright yellow vest, a walkie-talkie, and a large red stop sign, I began to stand at the crosswalk in the afternoons, rain or shine, cold or hot. Eventually some light administrative duties were added to my role. What follows is a record of my experience over the first five months or so. Without Piper at my side (as I explained in my first book, *The Missing Handle*—how is that for a shameless plug?!—Piper was very much a therapy dog, she would listen to my babbling and not say a word, though if she did talk one of us would have to go) I really had no one to talk to except myself. What follows is what I heard.

* * *

A question well worth asking, and, in many ways, the reason for my writing this in the first place is: Why should I read this book? Will it answer that proverbial question of why the chicken crossed the road?

When it comes to questions of "Why?" our responses are often subject to the values we hold most dear (more on this in Chapter Three). Our motivations for how we are living our lives (crossing the road, so to speak) are built on the faith and fortitude that enables and empowers us to get up in the morning and make our day what it is.

As such, the question of "Why did the chicken cross the road?" is not as important to me as is the question of "What did the chicken do once on the other side?" That is, in many ways, the primary purpose of this book. It is meant to provide some very specific suggestions for how we can make this journey we call life as intentional and meaningful as it can be, for us and for the world at large. How can we make a difference in this world that will make it a better and safer place for us and for our children?

It is my hope that as you read these "confessions" you will find the clarity in your own thinking to ensure that every step you take will lead you in the direction you want to go.

There are times when I look around at the school and how I seem to be received by the staff and the teachers (most of whom do not seem to know what to do with me). I often think they see me as some kind of "special needs service project." However, I learned a long time ago that judging the merit of one's life by what others may or may not think of or about you is not worth the effort. In fact, it is draining. I just smile at their comments, and go back to copying their worksheets for the students or laminating whatever it is that they deem to be of such importance. Having lived in the protective bubble of the Jewish world as a congregational and community leader, expected to know about and respond to all that matters even before it happened, perfectly, I find this a very different world. However, it is one that I am enjoying and that has caused me to think about living life as it is meant to be lived. As with every sermon I have ever given, this book is really for myself more than anything else. I have learned much on my corner and look forward to the chapters that are yet to be written.

* * *

I have been purposely "concisely ambiguous" when it comes to describing the school at which I work. The anonymity is meant to:

- Prevent me from embarrassing the school (staff, faculty, students) any more than I already do. I joke about wanting to be voted the most obnoxious crossing guard in the area. And, when I sometimes cover the morning shift, I think I come close. My "Get in there and learn something good" is usually met with looks that are far from welcoming, especially from the older students. But the parents like it when, at the end of the day, I cajole the students to "Go home, do your homework, go to bed early and give your parents a break!"

- Emphasize how fluid the position is. Even as one moment leads to the next, so is each independent in and of itself. Many of the confessions may have been true one day, but not the next. What happened at one particular moment is not necessarily descriptive of any other. Is not life, however, much the same?

- Suggest that what follows applies to any school on any corner. These confessions are not meant to be critical comments regarding any person or place. The confessions are meant to enable us to stand tall and steady in the midst of our own journeys, and get across the road safely.

Chapter One

The Invisible Man

My shift runs from around 3:00ish p.m. to 3:35ish p.m. I say "ish" because the traffic (of cars and students) is not always consistent. I usually arrive around 2:50 p.m. Though I am full of all sorts of energy and want to say "hello," etc., for the most part, the people in the office are otherwise occupied. Parents calling with changing pick-up plans, teachers trying to figure out who is supposed to be going where, the students sometimes as confused as everyone else, these are, as one of the office people once put it: "the worst 40 minutes of my life!" But they do it day in and day out, and always with a smile. I learned very quickly that my best approach to things would be to get in and get out. Like the proverbial "invisible man" I do my best to get to where I have to go without leaving a wake. The school has to shut down for the day. I am the last thing the staff needs (or wants!) to worry about.

So, it is off to my corner.

That I learned to see myself as the invisible man is something that followed me to the corner as well.

- I joke that I am more of a crossing facilitator than a crossing guard as my stop sign seems, more often than not, to be seen as a suggestion than a command to the drivers and/or the students. I can only do my best and hope that no one (myself included) gets hit.

- Though I try to acknowledge each and every person crossing with a greeting of some sort, the normal response I get from those who do not avert their eyes is usually a blank stare.

- Yes, there are those who say, "Thank you" and/or make a passing remark about the weather, etc. However, even in those moments I am anonymous. I know that many are appreciative of what I am trying to do, but I am an anonymous being. Over the first five months only one person introduced himself.

I know that sounds harsh. The parents and students, for the most part, are friendly. However, it is clear that they all have much more important things on their minds. I am in that moment . . . they are on their way to the next.

On the one hand, there is no reason to expect much more. After all, the parents and the students are focused on a very particular mission: reuniting and getting home. On the other hand, however, especially as in my previous life as senior rabbi of a large congregation I had been at the center of the whirlwind, I was, at first, taken aback. And yet, the experience has been good for me as it has led me to contemplate:

- What does it take to be noticed in life?

- How important should that notice be?

- What should we be striving to accomplish?

- How do we know when our life is well lived?

- Is anyone really ever "invisible"?

Truth be told, few of us will be remembered in/through history beyond the generation or two that we touch. Even if, and it is rare indeed, that a building or a street is named after us, still, our destiny is not to be all that present in this world as it is to come. Depressing? Does that mean that life is meaningless? If there is no guarantee of immortality in the here and now what does that mean regarding our connection to the "there and then?"

Piper was not with me, so I had to ask these questions of myself!

Even as the questions began to form, I was reminded of a passage from a classical rabbinic text, *Pirke Avot*, which compiles significant statements passed down to us from our ancestors. In *Pirke Avot* 4:1 we read, in the name of Ben Zoma:

- Who is wise? The one who learns from all people.

- Who is mighty? The one who subdues his passions.

- Who is rich? The one who is satisfied with his portion.

- Who is honored? The one who honors others.

And, as I thought about these questions and their answers, I realized that being invisible might not be such a bad thing!

WHO IS WISE?

As the school year came to an end and the revelry of graduations filled the air, the administrator of the school at which I work posted the following (I do not know if it is hers, or she found it someplace else) on Facebook:

> *A big shout out to all the kids who didn't win an award, make honor roll, and barely made it through the school year. A big hug to the moms, dads, grandparents, caregivers, and foster parents that stuck by them as they maneuvered the school year.*
>
> *To the kids that didn't get invited to prom, didn't get a scholarship to college, and perhaps have to go straight to work out of high school . . . you are still worthy of a pat on the back and a Facebook post with people talking about how amazing you are!*
>
> *Some kids have to work twice as hard as other students just to get a C. We see your resilience, kindness, creativity, and generosity. We see your hard work and your achievements deserve recognition.*

From my experience, some of those kids turned out to be the wisest people that I have ever met.

What is wisdom? How do we measure it? Are the only people worth noticing those who have a plethora of letters indicating the degrees they have received after their names? History books do note examples of brilliant entrepreneurs and inventors who never finished school. However, for the most part, those examples are cited as the exceptions that prove the rule that the wisest are those who succeed in the more traditional paths of Ivy League schools and advanced graduate programs.

Ever need someone to help fix a critical flaw in your HVAC, plumbing, automobile, etc.? Who you gonna call?

So, who is wise, and worth noting for their wisdom? How did they get that way?

I will suggest that the wisest people are not necessarily the ones with the most letters after their names (I have a number I could list, but I know how stupid I can sometimes be so I do not!). The wisest people that I know are the ones who find meaning and purpose in what they do to make this world a better place. They start with the people around them, appreciating everyone they meet for who they are and how they are contributing to this world in which we live. They make it a point to seek meaningful relationships with those that they meet. They realize that what many would call "simple wisdom" is often the most profound.

Remember the very beginning of the pandemic lockdowns? Even as the doctors and first responders were lauded, deservedly, for their ability to help us with the threats that were out there, it was the front-line workers who rose like cream to the top of the glass (whether we saw our situation as "half empty" or "half full"). The front-line workers were the ones who enabled us to zig and zag around the threats and the structured responses that were put into place. They helped us to survive and thrive. And, they did what they did not just for the paycheck. They did it because they saw it as their mission. Their mission, vision, and values, the core of their wisdom, were shared with us up close and personal. And I do believe that we learned more about life and how it should be lived from them than any statistic that may have been flashed up on the TV screen.

So, who is wise? I would suggest that the wisest among us are those who are aware of what they do not know, but take the time and energy to connect with those who do. I have often described our world as being a community broken down into any number of communities of communities: large groups consisting of many smaller associations. All of us are members of many different cohorts. The wise among us recognize these levels of connection and strive to strengthen the ties that bind us together. The more we engage with others and learn from them, the wiser we become. Our knowledge base increases exponentially.

So far, what I have offered probably sounds fairly mundane. However, wisdom need not be obscure or esoteric. In fact, the deepest wisdom is the opposite. The deepest wisdom is that which brings us together with others.

Who is wise? The one who learns from all people.

WHO IS MIGHTY?

Who rules your world? I, without joking, have known that "a happy wife is a happy life," which has made my life most pleasurable. And, in every professional position that I have had, I have made it a point, regardless of organizational tables, board structures, or the culture of the particular organization, to make sure that I was connected with the maintenance staff. They are the people without whom we could not function. Position does not confer power or prestige, it demands responsibility.

Where (with whom) does power lie?

I will suggest that real strength is not to be found in physical prowess or one's position on any cultural food chain. Real power, the kind of power that enables us to live every day as if it were our last, fully and completely, comes from our ability to always remain focused on our mission, vision, and values while striving to construct realistic expectations of ourselves and others.

Power is a product of the relationships we build with those around us. It emerges as a byproduct of how we influence, or are influenced by, those with whom we interact. Classically, our understanding of power is hierarchical: one person controls another. However, real power is not hierarchical, it is relational.

An example of a classical hierarchical understanding of power is as follows: When I have the stop sign in my hand at the corner I (supposedly) have power over who gets to go where and when. Sometimes people obey my directions, sometimes they do not. Those who "obey" are influenced by my presence and the purpose of my actions. Those who do not (and there have been several times when I have wanted to throw my stop sign at a car that breezed through the cross walk while I was signaling for them to stop—but I did not as I did not want to damage the sign) send a different message. In either case, when looked at hierarchically, one side wins over the other.

Real power, relational power as I would call it, is different. Real power is that which empowers us, the others in our lives, and the world at large. Real power emerges when we silently hold the hand of someone who is hurting, or when we hug and laugh with someone who realizes how much they have for which to be grateful. Real power is when we are there for, and with, others. It is not controlling or manipulative. Real power binds us together as one.

Most people are obsessed with hierarchical power. We live in a competitive culture where our value is measured by whether we win or lose. This kind of power is selfish and consuming. Like the carrot before a donkey or the spinning wheel in a hamster cage, one is in constant pursuit of something they will never be able to catch. It is intoxicating and addictive, but never satisfying.

Relational power is that which gives us a sense of accomplishment. Independent of whether or not we get credit for what we do, we know that we have been impactful and that is enough. Real power is when we put our competitive ego to the side and see how much more we accomplish when we strive to be part of that which is bigger than ourselves.

The whole concept of hierarchical power leads to bullying and abuse. Relational power, the type of power that emerges when we subdue our personal passions for recognition, leads to might—the kind of strength that enables us to live every day fully and completely. Especially because, by definition, it compels us to look out for the other guy as much as for ourselves, it is what gets us across the road.

Hierarchical power may lay heavily on our minds. It can be overwhelming, controlling, and a force that we seem to always be butting our heads against. How we deal with it may determine how we survive from day to day. Relational power is what enlivens our souls and gives us what we need to thrive.

Who is mighty? He who subdues his passions.

WHO IS RICH?

One of my favorite pastimes while waiting for my charges to arrive is to count cars. I do an unscientific survey almost every day of the Mercedes, BMWs, Teslas, Audis, Infinities, Lincolns, Cadillacs, and other luxury cars that pass me by. Yes, there are a few Toyotas, Chevys, and other economy cars, etc. that make their way down the road. However, I am amazed that the majority of vehicles are so "special." Many of them cost more than what I paid for my first house, and even more cost at least two to three times as much as my parents paid for theirs. Is it all a matter of inflation?

I have not tried to stop anyone and ask. Arizona has a permitless carry gun law, and there are all too many shootings, especially from road rage, already. However, I would venture to guess that few of the purchases and/or leases were utilitarian.

Why do we crave such abundance? Is avarice so embedded in our being that it is what enables, ennobles and empowers us? There is an irony to the desire to have only the best and brightest when it comes to cars. If it is to impress ourselves or others, the effort fails. Maybe if the car is parked in our driveway for all to see—but who would want to leave it out and exposed to the weather? Besides, most of these cars have tinted windows and you cannot see who is driving! Not much of an impression, is it?

So, what is it with the desire for wealth? We are raised by the popular culture and conventional wisdom to believe that our worth is to be measured by the quantity and quality of the stuff we accumulate over the course of our lifetime. Does it really bring prestige? I have done, over the course of my career, probably close to 2,000 funerals. I never saw a Brinks truck follow the hearse. The kind of wealth that is measured in terms of the stuff we call our own is far from enduring. It actually goes nowhere.

Some may think that that is easy to say. After all, I live a comfortable life in my own home, have more leftovers in the freezer than some have in their refrigerator for a month, and my wife can spoil our grandchildren with whatever they want or need. However, I know what it is like to be hungry. There were times in my life when, if I gathered the courage to go to the store, I had to decide if I wanted milk or juice as I could not afford them both. My kids used to make fun of me for shopping at Walmart, Kmart, and Kohl's with coupons. Until one day, when I had had enough, I asked them if they liked the sneakers they were wearing or the brand-name jeans hanging in their closets, all of which were possible only because I lived and shopped as I did. I will grant you that I have a lot of stuff (books and clothes to last me the rest of my life and then some). However, it is not the stuff that brings happiness, it is everything else that surrounds it. I am not sure that I ever really knew if/when I would/should have been considered as "poor." However, the happiest days were not dependent upon what I had as much as what I was doing with what I did or did not have.

There is a great deal of wisdom in this text concerning the measure of one's wealth. I was once taught that the definition of the word "utopia" is "no place." The reason given is that every time one thinks they have achieved such perfection, there is always one more step they could take. It is the same with our possessions. As soon as we think we have it all, there is one more thing that comes to mind.

What does it take for us to say that we have enough? Maybe it is understanding that it is enough to have what we do, that happiness is not achieved by having what you want as much as by wanting what you have.

I often told my kids that if they judge their "worth" by what others think or say about them, they will never be satisfied. Only when they can be content with what they have and who they are will they be able to step forward and continue to grow into what they still can become.

Success should not be conditional on what we think we have that we can call our own, or on what others think about us (or our stuff!).

What is success? What is it that can help us appreciate our real worth, the sources of wealth that are ours? As a quote often attributed to Ralph Waldo Emerson puts it:

> To laugh often and much; to win the respect of the intelligent people and the affection of children; to earn the appreciation of honest critics and endure the betrayal of false friends; to appreciate beauty; to find the best in others; to leave the world a bit better, whether by a healthy child, a garden patch, or a redeemed social condition; to know that one life has breathed easier because you have lived here. This is to have succeeded.

WHO IS HONORED?

It is part of our DNA to want to be recognized for who we are and what we do. And there are some who let that DNA get the better of them, who seem to be obsessed with knowing that others are aware of them. However, if the pursuit of such honor is the source of whether or not we feel validated I am quite sure we never will. So, what do we do? How do we strike a balance?

I do not believe that life is meaningless, or that we are invisible even when we think we might be. What I believe is that we must carefully examine our expectations of ourselves and others so that we have a realistic picture of life and how it might best be lived. The most realistic picture needs to include our presence.

Consider this famous rabbinic story, which I have paraphrased:

> When David was being pursued by Saul's army (Saul was a bit jealous of and paranoid about David, considering him a threat to his position as king), he fled into the wilderness. Hiding in a cave, he put his hand down and found the ground crawling with spiders. What to do? He thought about trying to kill as many as he could but decided that he would let them be, hoping they would let him alone as well. As the story goes, they must have, because it continues with David awakening in the morning to the sound of soldiers searching the wilderness looking for him. As they approached his cave, they kept walking, agreeing that there was no way he could be in there as the opening was covered with a very large, intact, spider web. And so, because he recognized the worth of even the smallest and seemingly insignificant creepy crawler, David lived to tell the tale.

There are other versions of this story, and other examples involving different characters over the course of different time periods. The point? The point is simple: everyone and everything counts. Had the spiders been killed, chances are David would have been as well. I have always told people that strange as it may seem, the classic Christmas movie, *It's A Wonderful Life* with James Stewart, is a very Jewish movie. What would the world have been like without George Bailey? Similarly, what would our world be like without our presence? We all are important in our own way. We are intrinsic to the workings of the space-time continuum. What about all the bad people and the horrible things that sometimes occur? That is for my next book. Let's worry about ourselves first. Or, as the passage teaches us, about the others in our lives, ensuring that we are there for them as we need to be.

I will grant you that some of this sounds hard. It can be difficult to find the confidence to live life in relationship with (there for) others because they are there, and not for our own aggrandizement. However, that is the point. The most important person to be concerned about is the one we see in the mirror when we wake up in the morning and when we go to sleep at night. And to be proud of that reflection takes wisdom, strength, an understanding of our self-worth, and the awareness of the fact that everyone and everything (including, if not especially ourselves) has a role to play in this world.

Even if/when we may feel ourselves to be invisible, that is only a mirage. If we examine our expectations of ourselves and others, I do believe that we will find much more to our presence (whatever that might be) and life itself to be more satisfying and enjoyable.

As I write, my vest and stop sign are in storage for the summer. Talk about invisibility! However, I am sure that neither I or they will get dusty!

- Why did the chicken cross the road?
- Do you think anyone even noticed?
  - If so, what do you think they noticed the most?
    - Does it matter?
  - If not, why not?
    - Does it matter?

Change the word "chicken" in this first series of questions to "you" and answer them.

- How are your answers the same/different?

- Why are you living the life that you are?
- How many roads have you had to cross in order to get to where you are today?

- What impact is your life having on our world (especially the little corner that you inhabit)?
- What is the impact that you would like it to have?

- Given the invisibility factor (not everyone notices us for what/who we think we are!) that exists in life, from where do we get the mission, vision, and values to stay on the path that we have chosen?
- What drives us to "cross the road"?

Chapter Two

Ten Seconds? I'd Take Five!

WHY DID THE CHICKEN cross the road? What did she do once she got there?

A little background: Our younger son, Ricky, was born prematurely. He spent six weeks in the NICU and received a great deal of special attention after that. The year we moved to Tucson, he was entering the fourth grade. To say that the transition was hard on him is an understatement. By January, he could not take it anymore and began running away from school. Fortunately, he always came home (which was across the street). However, the trauma left its mark. We pulled him from that school and enrolled him in the local Jewish day school, where he completed fourth through eighth grade, and then he went back to public school. In the summer of 2017, at the age of 28, Ricky died. How I responded to that time is reflected in my first book, The Missing Handle *(this is not a shameless plug, but an explanation for why I am not going any further with that theme here). And yet, there was a moment while standing on my corner when those days were relived a little too up front and personal.*

Shortly after I began to work my afternoon shifts, I was asked to fill in for the morning crossing guard, who had a conflict. It was not hard to rearrange my schedule, and I knew that there would be times when I would ask that person to return the favor and cover the afternoon shift. The morning crowd was mostly people I recognized from the afternoon and the responsibility was pretty much the same. I was joking with the students, at least with those who recognized me and seemed to stare quizzically at me, wondering why I was there in the morning, telling them to "Get in there and learn something good." And then there was a call on the walkie-talkie: "We have a runner!" It seems that one of the students had had enough even before the day began and was trying to go home. The flashback was immediate. All I could think of was Ricky's face when he showed up at our door or I caught him cutting through a wash. The pain was palpable. I was so engaged in the flashback that I neglected to see the father and son standing near me waiting to cross the street. "I am so sorry," I said. "I kind of got distracted." "That is OK," the father said. "I got an extra ten seconds with my son. That is worth everything." Ten seconds, I thought to myself. I would take five! I finished my shift and drove around for a long while before going home. In the car, I remembered the moment. In retrospect, I remember feeling numb.

Ten seconds? Five seconds? Forever? What would I say? What would I want to ensure that he knew? What are the essential responsibilities that we have to our children? I wrestled with those questions many times over the next few months. Though the obvious desire was to let Ricky know how much he is/was loved and missed, I also wondered if I had fulfilled my greater obligation as a father, as it is spelled out in the Jewish tradition. If I was more of a communicator, I would maybe try to have some sort of discussion with our older son to see how I fared. What follows is what I hope he, and others, would find helpful as a guide to what could and should be said to/with their children . . . whether it is ten, or five, or how many seconds that conversation might take.

So, what does the Jewish tradition say? In the Babylonian Talmud (a collection of rabbinic teachings regarding Jewish law compiled around the 5th century C.E.) we are taught (Kiddushin 29a):

A father is obligated to:

- circumcise his son

- to redeem him
- to teach him Torah
- to marry him off
- to teach him an occupation

- And [But] some say: to teach him to swim.

The rest of this chapter will revolve around just what those responsibilities look like when translated into the 21st century.

The first three items on the list are very parochial and this is not meant to be a review of "Basic Judaism," though that is the language in which I speak. In essence, these first three items reflect the command to bring one's child into the covenant and ensure that he has the way open to him to be an engaged member of the Jewish People. How is that to be accomplished? Especially considering all the variables and attractions that are out there? I would suggest it is by living as you would want your children to live.

I lived in Buffalo, New York during the 1990s, the decade during which many of the parents at my school were probably born. It was an interesting and challenging time. Politically, the Christian Coalition was actively engaged in putting candidates in as many races as it could. Most did not succeed, until there was a change in policy. The Coalition decided to abandon the larger races (such as Congress, etc.), and work from the bottom up, pursuing seats, especially, on local school boards. The strategy included staging "stealth candidates" (people who hid their real agenda until after they were elected) on many of the ballots. As such, there were many issues regarding the teaching of and about religion (particular religions and religiosity in general) that were raised that had not been addressed in the past. And the "discussions" got noisier and noisier. One local school board decided to be proactive and put a committee together to draft a policy that would address the teaching about religion in public schools. Because of my position as rabbi of a local synagogue, I became one of the representatives of the Jewish community.

Participating in, and observing the dynamics of, the work of the committee was fascinating. I learned more about human nature than I wanted to! The most intense discussions reflected the purpose of the committee to draft a proposal regarding the teaching ABOUT religion, and the desire of many of the participants to ensure that the schools would actually teach religion (what they would expect the church to which they did not belong to teach their children). Whereas in the Jewish community many parents sent their children to synagogue religious schools after regular school and on weekends, the general community expected the public schools to do that work for them. The best example was when one of the members of the committee took issue with the section dealing with the approach to different holidays: should they be recognized? . . . taught about? . . . celebrated? What about music? I said that I had no problem with a concert that included religious Christmas music, if it were held in March! My point was made, and I heard about "it" in the parking lot afterward. Why do I say, "it"? Because their point was not so much about the content of any particular concert as it was that they thought the role of the schools was to teach their children what they did not. They expected the schools to teach their children the meaning, message, and importance of observing Christmas. The passage I quoted above from the Talmud suggests the exact opposite; it is we, the parents, who have the primary responsibility to teach our children the basic values by which we should be living our lives. And such lessons cannot be taught only in words. Such lessons are "life lessons," learned only by/through doing.

I remember vividly one of the first weeks that I was in my first position as an assistant rabbi in a large congregation. We were gathered at a collation following the service. I was chatting with the senior rabbi when a woman came over and in a very passionate voice said in no uncertain terms: "Did you see all those children at the service this morning, talking and playing and running around in the back of the sanctuary?" Her intent was a complaint. However, my senior, who had life tenure, responded with a huge smile on his face, "Yes, wasn't it beautiful! Maybe if you had brought your children once in a while they would still be coming too!"

The responsibility of parents to raise their children is not to be part-time caretakers. It is a full-on obligation (though in retrospect I would hope we would see it as an honor and privilege to have had the trust and investment our children make in us!) to go beyond giving them life and teach them how to live as well. That can only be accomplished through example. There is a teaching in the Jewish tradition that should one find their parent and their teacher in mortal danger and is called upon to save them, if we can only save one, the teacher comes first. Why? Again, because more important than the giving of life is teaching that (and every other!) life how to live. Our text would have it that we (as parents) might be that teacher as well, one and the same.

Our text, however, is not concerned with just telling our children what we want them to learn, it is "obsessed" with our doing what we expect of them . . . first! Children are very perceptive. They learn quickly which parent to go to when they have a "special request." And, they know when a parent is joking or "acting out" (OK, lying!). Strange as it may sound, our primary responsibility to our children is to be responsible (true) to ourselves. If we want them to develop honorable values such as honesty, integrity, and generosity, etc., then we have to model such behavior ourselves.

Going back to that committee on the teaching about religion in the public schools, the parents who had the biggest problems with the policy were those who expected the schools to teach their children what they did not. Perhaps that is why some of the problems we are having today have become so political and personal. We cannot expect the schools to do what we do not, and then hold them accountable for doing what is right and best. If we teach, by example, what we believe and expect from ourselves as we live our lives from day to day, then we will find the schools being able to focus on what they are supposed to be doing: helping our children develop basic life skills for success. Let the teachers teach, and let us do our part as the important factors in the equation that we are.

And then the text from the Talmud continues: *To marry him off.*

Many of us are familiar with the old joke about when life begins. The priest says, at conception. The minister says, at birth. The rabbi says, when the dog dies and the kids move out of the house. This concern in our text is not rooted in that joke. The concern revolves around the idea that we enable our children to have hopes and prayers and dreams, a vision of a future that they want to be part of.

I can remember innumerable late-night conversations when I was in undergraduate school about how none of us would ever get married much less bring children into this wanton and forsaken world. It would not be fair to them. Fortunately, DNA, hormones, and common sense prevailed and most of us did partner up and pursue building families (personally, or playing our part in our extended families). The difference between these stages of our lives was the ability to see and believe in the opportunities the future holds for us, and how important it was to share that vision with other living souls.

Yes, we all have moments when we wonder. And, unfortunately, too many of us have "hells" that we have lived through. However, I believe that this text is trying to teach us that qualitatively, if not quantitatively, life is good, and worth living. And, to empower someone to partner up is to enable them to believe the same. One of the most enduring lessons a parent can provide a child is the ability to look forward, to hope and dream and imagine a future filled with everything they want. Knowing that things may not (will not?) work out exactly as planned, life is found most meaningful in the journey more than the destination. Having an image of the future that is worth pursuing, regardless of the changes that we know will come, is a life well lived.

Perhaps the best translation of this element of the responsibilities a parent has to their children is to teach them to smile.

And then the text continues: *To teach him an occupation.*

For the most part, the expectation that we place on our children is far from whether or not to go to college, but, rather, to choose which college they want to attend. We may coax a preferred major out of them; however, we are usually more concerned about the education they are going to get than what they might end up doing with that education. Let them pick anything, as long as it is an honorable profession.

A quick joke:

> A Jewish politician has been elected to the office of president of the United States. As he plans the inauguration with his staff, he ensures that there will be adequate seating for his family, especially his mother, who always taught him that he could be whatever he wanted to be. As the day for the inauguration approaches, he calls his mother to tell her that Air Force One will be at the airport to pick her up and fly her to Washington for the ceremony. "Oh, but it is so far away, and flying is never easy, and besides, the Mahjongg group is set to meet that day and I do not want to miss it," his mother complains. "But mom," he protests, "I am going to be inaugurated as the president of the United States, you must come." Realizing that she cannot get out of it, she acquiesces and prepares for the trip. There she sits, in the front row, next to the immediate past president. As the ceremony proceeds, the past president turns to the woman and asks who she is and why she is there, etc. She points to the stage and says, "You see that man being sworn in as president? That is my son." "You must be most proud of him!" the past president exclaims. "Oh, of course I am, but you see the man three seats down from here? That is my other son. He is a doctor!"

That is a joke? Sometimes I laugh. However, all too often I have seen such sentiment acted out, forever changing family dynamics irreparably. Perhaps that is why the last clause of the text, *And some say: to teach him to swim*, would be better translated as "*But some say*" (which is not so unusual given the Hebrew construction of the phrase). That is, the primary responsibility we have as parents is to teach our children how to survive, how to weather life's storms and always stay afloat. President? Doctor? Electrician? Plumber? Landscaper? Which is more important: what our children might do with their lives? . . . or, how they are going to live their lives? Which is more important: having our children fulfill some ego-driven (on our part) expectation regarding their fame and fortune? . . . or, enabling them to ensure that what they do will make the world a better place and that they will always be able to look in the mirror and smile, knowing that they did their best?

For the most part, I have no idea what the parents of the students that I help cross the road do for a living. A few come from work in scrubs, or a uniform of some sort. But, on the whole, they could be just about anything. Their children are the same. I have little to no idea what it is those students are dreaming about being or becoming, or if such goals are even on their radar. And yet, what I would be most interested in learning is what the parents are teaching their children. What kind of values are they modeling? What are the lessons their children are learning in those precious "ten seconds" that they have together? Are those conversations happening at all?

A favorite joke that we like to tell, that has innumerable answers, all of which become the punch line to begin with is: Why did the chicken cross the road? As I stand on my corner facilitating the students and their parents on their journeys, my question is the same: Why are they crossing the road? What is their purpose? What do they want to achieve? Are they taking those ten (or even five) seconds that they will never get back to make an impression that will last a lifetime?

When it comes to questions of "Why?" our responses are often subject to the values we hold most dear. Our motivations for how, and the manner in which, we are living our lives (crossing the road, so to speak) is built on the faith and fortitude that enables and empowers us to get up in the morning and make our day what it is.

As such, the question of "Why did the chicken cross the road?" is not as important to me as the question: "What did the chicken do once on the other side?" What did the chicken do in those first ten (five?) seconds once safely across the road? How can we make this journey we call life as intentional and meaningful as it can be, for us, and for the world at large? How can we make a difference in this world that will make it a better and safer place for us and for our children?

- Why did the chicken cross the road?
- Do you think she was more concerned with where she was coming from, or where she was going?
  - Would it make a difference?

Change the word "chicken" (and "she") in this first series of questions to "you" and answer them.

- How are your answers the same/different?

- Have you ever felt like you did not know if you were "coming" or "going"?
- How did that impact what you were doing at that particular moment?

- If you had the opportunity to "do it again" what would you like to have heard your parent(s) teach you?
- What do you think you should be teaching your children?
  - Are you?
  - Why? Why not?

- I always pause for a minute on Father's Day and think about all the Facebook posts about the absolutely best and brightest and perfect fathers that are out there. Most of us (fathers, mothers, teachers, etc.) are far from the perfect images that these posts describe. And yet, even if not the best, what does it mean to try our best?
- What kind of "chicken" would that make us?

Chapter Three

The Celtics?

One of my favorite pastimes while standing at my corner, besides listening and "dancing" to classic rock, is reading the T-shirts that the students are wearing. Culturally illiterate as I am (I do not watch a great deal of TV), it is from the slogans and messages with which the students (and parents!) adorn themselves that I can sort of keep up with what is going on in the world. Though I am often taken aback, like the day that, while the Suns were in the NBA playoffs and a student came to school all in green Celtics clothing. I commented on this and received a blank stare—in fact, the student had to look down at his shirt to figure out what I was talking about. But most of the time I just "read it and weep."

And yet, what those messages mean, and what they are trying to say to those who see them, is very much something about which a comment or two is necessary.

Most people dress the way they do to make a statement that they may or may not care about how they look, and/or to ensure that they are being transparent about their values. A couple of years ago, when visiting a physical therapist, I wore ASU shorts, a U of Az shirt, and a Syracuse hat. The PT just looked at me and said, "Couldn't make up your mind today?" I had to think for a moment regarding what he was talking about. I was wearing what I had on because it was clean and at the top of the drawer. However, he obviously thought otherwise! What was the statement I was trying to make? Was there one?

For the most part, we are defined by the values that we hold to be guiding principles. In fact, I would go so far as to say that our religion is defined by what we hold to be of ultimate value, which is then expressed through the rituals that we observe which reflect those core beliefs (guiding principles). In terms of our individuality, such values and rituals emerge from a variety of sources, including family, friends, and community, etc. However, they are also very much influenced by the cultural context in which we live, and the "civil religion" (that which we are told to hold as an ultimate value by self-appointed or accepted authorities) in which we are immersed.

Consider (broad brushstrokes admitted): As nomadic society transitioned into a more agrarian lifestyle, and villages began to emerge, it was not uncommon (in fact, often expected) that the building plan would include a "High Place" (worship center) as the most prominent structure in the layout. Later, one would find the church as the tallest building and centerpiece of the settlement. And it was the church that defined the standards and expectations of the then world that the people inhabited. It was faith (even if it was the pretense of faith) that gave the people fortitude.

As life began to get more complex, the civil authorities began to take their place at the center as well. Kings built their castles as magnets for the settlement of villages around them, and in the then "still more modern times," courthouses and government offices stood as the center of most inhabited areas. With this change came a secularization of society as well. Values competing with the church often became dominant.

Then came the industrial revolution and the factory took over as the defining structure of the urban settlement. Manufacturing and commercial goals rallied the people to the quest for a better life. What was good and/or would make you happy was defined by the stuff we could acquire. Chickens in the pot and cars in the garage were the elements of our hopes and prayers and dreams. And, while we were there, commercial centers grew as well. The "downtown" became the commercial and, therefore, cultural center of our lives. Materialism (as a byproduct of capitalism and the emerging/strengthening market economy) became the foundation upon which people found "their mojo."

Throughout these transitions, which often snuck up on us, we, for the most part, retained whatever ethnic identity we had by the neighborhoods in which we chose, or were forced, to live. The myth of the melting pot was very much a driving force in how we were supposed to define ourselves. However, as acculturation led to assimilation, there was a certain sort of rebellion: the move to the suburbs where, even if ethnic neighborhoods might not be preserved (preservable), there was enough space between the houses that people were able to maintain their individuality, at least in theory.

It did not take long for suburbia to fracture and fragment any sense of real community. Bricks and mortar and neon signs and mannequins, and especially fast food that you did not even have to eat in the restaurant, transitioned into "The Mall," which put even more daylight between individual families, their neighbors, and their community. Life was centrifugal, it forced us to be, and grow, apart from each other.

Something was needed to bring us back together. So, the city center was resurrected. Meant to bring people together as one, the coliseum of old was resurrected in the city center in order to give people common cause. And life became a reflection of the sports that were the foundation of our faith and fortitude. In our world it seems that even more than politics, life itself has become a competitive contact sport.

How many people find their heroes and role models among sports celebrities, wanting to mimic their swagger and their lifestyle? It does not matter if their behavior is subject to "concern," such as domestic violence, or drug abuse, or anything else that would hold anyone else suspect. After all, look at what they can do at the plate, or on the field, etc. The more grossly overpaid a sports figure might be, the more he or she is cherished by their fans.

And, along with the worship of sports idols came the obsession with "celebrities," for the most part, people who are paid obscene amounts of money to pretend to be something they are not! So many stars of stage, screen, and the recording studio hold sway over what we wear, what we eat, where we bank, how we think, and for whom to vote. For the most part, their power is not derived from any significant moral accomplishment. We have forsaken any sense of objective truth for the influence of passing fads.

Just in case we are not fractured and fragmented enough, we now have the internet and the digital age to ensure that we are "together apart"... or, is it apartness that defines our togetherness? Consider the headlines regarding the impact of distance/remote learning for the first year or so of the pandemic had on our children, not to mention our labor force and its now redefined understanding of any kind of work ethic. "Quitting in place" seems to be more important than fulfilling one's assigned task with intention, purpose, and pride.

What has all this done to us? What have we become because of it?

I am not suggesting that we need to abandon the elements of modern society that make our world what it is. I enjoy running water, penicillin, and a safe, healthy food supply. My question is, what are the means and what are the ends? Have we somehow confused them, and therefore the substance of our lives as well? What I am questioning is who we are trying to be and how we want other people to see us.

A great deal of this came to a head the day I saw a woman coming to pick up her children in a shirt bearing the words "Spiritual Gangster" in large letters across the front. Not knowing that this was a women's clothing line (which she described as being primarily for yoga), I asked if her "banner" was meant to be threatening. Was she planning to kill me? That one would associate being a spiritual gangster with yoga appears to me to be a bit contradictory. However, it does raise an important question: How militant are we when it comes to our beliefs? How do those beliefs then impact on our relationships with others? Do the billboards that we have become reflect the core values that motivate us to live our lives as we do? Or, have the billboards begun to impact, influence, and define the essence of who we are?

A story that has been told in any number of places in any number of different versions goes something like this:

> One evening a rabbi, puzzled by what and where life had brought him, decided to go out for a walk. As he wandered through the town in which he lived, he encountered a man in a uniform standing guard outside the home of a wealthy family. The rabbi asked the guard casually, "Who do you work for?" The guard answered politely, telling the rabbi the name of the family who had hired him. Then the guard asked the rabbi, "And who do you work for?" The rabbi thought intently before answering the guard. He was unsure of what the correct answer should be but knew that the question was what he had been pursuing along the path he had been exploring. He answered not with what the guard was expecting, but with a question of his own. He asked the guard, "Would you be willing to work also for me?" The guard answered quickly, "Of course I would. But what would be my duty?" The rabbi replied with a smile, "To ask me continually who I work for!"

Or, to put the story in the context of "The Celtics," what is the essence of our being? We are known for who we are by what we do. What are our clothes—or better yet, the way we are living our lives—saying about us to ourselves and others?

Shortly after reading that story for the first time, I changed the screen saver on my computer to the Hebrew phrase that asks, "Who do you work for?" I also made index cards with the first letters of those words and placed them in strategic places. People knew all of that was meant to be a motivator for me, but, until the week before I left the congregation in Tucson, not one person ever asked me what the phrase or the letters meant, or why I had them positioned as I did. I was not trying to be secretive; I was trying to stay on track and ensure that I knew what I was wearing (literally and figuratively) and what it said about me to other people. The rabbi in the story knew just by looking at the guard, from the way he was dressed, that he worked for someone else. What does the way people see us say about who we work for?

So, what are the values that we hold to be most central to our lives and the intentionality with which we are trying to live them? How are they expressed in and through our deeds, the clothing with which we adorn ourselves? What and where is our "High Place"? Are we even aware of what we say we think we believe?

This is not a matter of worrying about what other people think about us. Those who live their lives worried mostly (only!) about what others think are not going to get very far in or with their lives. This is a matter of focusing on what we think about ourselves, and how we are known for who and what we want those selves to be.

Why did the chicken cross the road? What did she do when she got there?

I would hope that she crossed the road because *she* wanted to and saw each movement/moment as an intentional step along her journey. And, when she got to the other side of the road, I hope she was recognized for what she had accomplished as the "person" that she was . . . and felt good about what she had accomplished as well.

I remember telling that young man in the Celtics shirt, jokingly, that I should probably let him cross the street by himself (no one appreciates my sense of humor as much as I do). But I crossed him, with pride, hoping that he would always be true to himself and what he believed: a die-hard Celtics fan . . . or comfortable in the shirt that he was wearing, no matter what anyone saw it as saying.

To paraphrase a famous passage from Jewish literature:

> The Rabbis used to say: I am God's creature and my neighbor is God's creature. My work is in the city, and his work is in the field. I rise early for work, and he rises early for work. He does not do what I do, neither do I do what he does. Lest you say one of us is better than the other, let us remember that we have been taught: One who brings a substantial offering and one who brings a

meager offering have equal merit in My eyes, as long as he directs his heart toward Me [God].

What we do and why we do it are considered to be one and the same. With clarity of purpose, life takes on a whole different dimension. It, and we, begin to mean something, to make an impact on this world to make it a better place.

I am not much of a sports fan. Living in Buffalo as we did during the '90s and experiencing the Bills losing four Super Bowls in a row cured me of being any kind of fan, much less a "super fan." And yet, I often wear a Bills hat, on which I receive innumerable comments. Remembering what it was like in year five—when we were praying that the Bills did not make it to the end!—I usually respond to any comment regarding the Bills with, "The trick to being a Bills fan is never expecting them to win a game. Then if they do, it is something special." I would suggest that that is a little bit of what this chapter is about: if we live life with intentionality, with vision, mission, and values, the journey itself will make it all worth it. And, if/when we are granted the gift of a special moment (and we are, though we do not always recognize them until they are over/gone), we will realize how much more special we really are.

Celtics fans or not!

- Why did the chicken cross the road?
  - What was she trying to accomplish?
  - What were those who saw her crossing thinking about her?

Change the word "chicken" (and "she") in this first series of questions to "you" and answer them.

- How are your answers the same/different?

- What values do you consider to be the most compelling in your life?

- How long does it take you to decide what you are going to wear each morning?
- As you "dress for success" what statement is your apparel making?
- When someone sees you "in all your glory" what do you want them to think about you?

- How influenced do you believe yourself to be by the "values" of our society?
- Do you find yourself following a particular fashion trend, or focusing on a particular way of doing something, because you saw a "celebrity" so engaged?

- If someone were to describe your mission, vision, and values based on the way you dress and the activities with which you are involved, what would they say?
- What would you like them to say about you?

- The chicken crosses the road and gets on with her life . . . one day someone has to write her epitaph . . . what would it read?
- What would you like yours to read?

Chapter Four

Dodgeball

As THE SCHOOL YEAR came to a close, we all started to focus on what opportunities the summer might afford us. When asked if I would miss my corner and the excitement that surrounded it, I usually responded, "NO," and explained that I had signed up for a dodge ball league so I could sharpen the skills I needed in order to survive the traffic! As I have said all too many times, there are too many people who think that the stop sign means slow down and aim for the guy in the yellow vest. I have become very agile on my feet and only got bumped once (so far)!

On the roughest days I always wonder if/how the worst offenders would be driving if they saw their children in the crosswalk. This led me to begin thinking about how we see the people with whom we share this world. What value do we place on their lives and their presence in ours? Traditionally there is a pretty basic and universal answer to that question. It is referred to as "The Golden Rule." You know it:

- Love your neighbor as yourself (Leviticus 19:18)
- That which is hateful to you do not do to another; that is the entire Torah, and the rest is its interpretation. Go study. (Judaism: Babylonian Talmud Shabbat 31a)

- In everything, do unto others as you would have them do unto you; for that is the Law and the Prophets. (Christianity: Matthew 7:12)

- None of you truly believes until he loves for his brother what he loves for himself (Islam: 40 Hadith 13)

- Lay not on any soul a load which you would not wish to be laid upon you, and desire not for any one the things you would not desire for yourselves. (Baha'i: Gleanings from the Writings of Baha'u'llah)

- One should never do that to another which one regards as injurious to one's own self. This, in brief, is the rule of dharma. (Hinduism: Brihaspati, Mahabharata 13.113.8)

- Hurt not others in ways that you yourself would find hurtful. (Buddhism: Udanavarga 5:18)

- In happiness and suffering, in joy and grief, we should regard all creatures as we regard our own self, and should therefore refrain from inflicting upon others such injury as would appear undesirable to us if inflicted upon ourselves. (Janism: Yugasastra)

- Ziong asked, "Is there a single saying that one may put into practice all one's life? The Master said, "That would be 'reciprocity': That which you do not desire, do not do to others. (Confucianism: The Analects of Confucius 15:24)

- Regard your neighbor's gain as your own gain, and your neighbor's loss as your own loss. (Taoism: Lao Tse's Treatise on the Response of the Tao)

- Ever mind the Rule of Three: Three times your acts return to thee. This lesson well, you must learn. You only get what you earn. (Wicca: The Rule of Three)

Many years ago, I brought these quotes to an adult education class that I was teaching. After unpacking a few of the quotes with which we were least familiar, I asked the class to break into small groups, analyze the passages, and prioritize them in terms of most compelling/powerful to least. About halfway through their discussions (which were very vociferous) I stopped the exercise and asked them what was wrong with what they were doing. Everyone "got it" at the same time. To evaluate and compare/contrast these passages with and against each other was the exact opposite of what they were teaching us regarding how life should be lived. How can we judge if, in the end, we want to be together as one?

What does/will/would it take for us to take this Golden Rule seriously and enable it to be a core (ultimate) value in our lives? For a couple of extra bucks, you can get a license plate here in Arizona with the caption, "Live the Golden Rule." But some of the people who have such plates are the most competitive players in my daily dodgeball game.

What does/will/would it take?

I will suggest that the first step is recognizing that the world does not revolve around us. Rather, it is we who are part of something greater than ourselves, the world at large. That is, we need a spiritual "Copernican Revolution" (Don't get the reference? Look it up!).

And that is a hard thing to accomplish. After all, weren't we taught (and teach our children) that we (they) are all that matters? I will never forget watching my children's kindergarten teacher (they both had the same one) ending circle time with the students standing and, while pointing to their chest, singing very loudly, to the tune of "Frère Jacques," "I am special, I am special, yes I am, yes I am. I am very special, I am very special, yes I am, yes I am." One time she had them end the song by pointing away from themselves, toward the other kids in the class, and sing, "So are you, so are you." However, from the looks on the kids' faces, I believe that led to confusion more than anything else. I guess the Golden Rule regarding who gets respect may not be as precious as we think!

Or perhaps we do need to begin with ourselves to take the first step. However, it needs to be taken in a slightly different direction than we are used to.

In essence, the Golden Rule is asking that we have compassion toward the others in our world. It wants us to believe in their worth the same way they believe in ours. In fact, I once heard the verse from Leviticus translated not as "Love your neighbor as yourself," but, rather, as "Love your neighbor the way they love you"! Do they? Sometimes it feels as if they do. Sometimes that seems like the farthest from the truth we could be. Maybe we should love our neighbor the way we want them to love us?! However, we must start somewhere. Rabbi Jonathan Sacks, as I understand his words to be a "paraphrase" of the Golden Rule, teaches, using the concept of *Chessed* ("covenantal love". . . "loving kindness"—a word that appears some 250ish times in the Bible):

> *Chessed* . . . is personal. We cannot care for the sick, bring comfort to the distressed or welcome a visitor impersonally. If we do so, it merely shows that we have not understood what these activities are . . . *Chessed* is an act of engagement . . . *Chessed* exists only in virtue of emotion, empathy, and sympathy, feeling-with and feeling-for. We act with kindness because we know what it feels like to be in need of kindness. We comfort the mourners because we know what it is to mourn. *Chessed* requires . . . emotional intelligence.

Chessed, pursuit of the Golden Rule, is personal, but it is also very selfish. To achieve any level of meaningful altruism, we have to start with ourselves, focusing on what makes life most meaningful for us and seeing how that impacts on how we interact (engage) with others.

Consider the following (which I have heard in many different versions from many different sources):

> The story is told of a rabbi and an abbot, whose chance (as if anything is really a matter of chance) encounter changed a world.
>
> In a little town in a faraway land, there was a little Jewish community led by a rabbi who had served for as long as anyone could remember. The rabbi was happy with his lot and content with what he saw as his future. However, his reputation for understanding and advice began to spread throughout the land and he found that he had little time to himself for study, or even just to

think. And, strange as it may sound, though embraced by so many people, he felt lonely. He decided he needed to make time for himself, so he began to take long walks in the woods surrounding his village at least once a week. Those walks enabled him to clear his mind and resume his work with confidence and compassion.

At the same time, just outside of that little village, high on a surrounding hill, there was an abbey that was known for its wine and its cheese. People would come from miles away to spend an afternoon high up on the hill, walk and talk with the monks, and return home with nourishment for body and soul. However, as the reputation of the abbey spread, the crowds grew too big for the monks to handle and they began to bicker among themselves regarding who was responsible for what, and how things "should" be getting done. The atmosphere changed, people stopped coming, and there were few, if any, who knocked at the door wanting to train as a novitiate. The abbot did not know what to do. He needed time to think and regain his sense of purpose. He decided he needed to make such time so he began to take long walks in the woods surrounding the abbey at least once a week.

What happened next? You guessed it! On one of those walks the rabbi and the abbot met. Though hesitant at first because they thought themselves to be from such different worlds, eventually they began to connect. At the end of that chance encounter, they planned to meet again, each yearning for the continuation of their conversation. As time went on, those walks/conversations became the essence of their being; they learned more about themselves than they knew that they could. The rabbi gained a sense of companionship, and the more he opened himself up to the abbot, the more the abbot shared with him, and the more at peace he felt to be with himself and the world as a whole. He had a friend.

And the abbot? As he poured his heart out to the rabbi and asked for advice regarding how to best proceed, the rabbi told him, "I do not have any simple fix that I can give you. However, I would suggest that you do not have to worry so much. I had a dream the other day in which I was told that one of the monks high on the hill was the Messiah." The abbot could not believe his ears, but if the rabbi said it, it must be true.

The abbot returned to the abbey and all the monks could see that there was something different about him. It did not take long for the pressure to mount and the abbot told the rest of the monks what the rabbi had said. They looked at each other and began to wonder. Could it be Thomas who was always tending to the garden? Was it John who prepared their meals with such care? The monks began to look at each other with a different eye. If the other was to be the Messiah, then the protocol was clear, there had to be a whole different attitude . . . there needed to be love. Slowly the atmosphere at the abbey changed and the happiness the monks once knew returned. The people who visited noticed a difference, and soon the abbey was more productive than it ever was, and there were more and more young men knocking at the door wondering if they might learn to join the order.

You shall love your neighbor as yourself!? Perhaps that is best understood as a command to love all the "others" in our lives as we would like to be loved. Are you the Messiah? If I treat you as such, will you treat me the same? What kind of world would we have if we really did the following:

- Try to talk with each other rather than at each other?

- Walked along side by side, rather than at arm's length, suspicious of manner and motive?

- Saw each moment as having the potential to change the world?

- Were able to cross the street without fearing that we would be hit?!

- Played catch instead of dodgeball?

When it comes to being selfish, I am often the first person in line! I want things to be different. I want the world to be as it should be, not as it is. And I want all of this now! How can any of that be accomplished? In the same way as avarice is at the core of all vice, so can that selfishness lead to a greater sense of altruism, if I see you as I would want you to see me . . . if I approach an intersection as if my kids are walking through the crosswalk.

- Why did the chicken cross the road?
  - Do you think that she would have preferred to cross alone, or with a companion?
  - Whom do you think she would prefer to have accompanying her?
  - Why?

Change the word "chicken" (and "she") in this first series of questions to "you" and answer them.

- How are your answers the same/different?

- Do you think that the Golden Rule is achievable?
- Is following the Golden Rule a sign of weakness or strength?
- If it is a guiding principle, how does it impact our sense of purpose and our "competitive edge" that drives us to succeed at what we do?

- Of the many versions of the rule that are listed above, which resonates the most with you?
- Why?

- I was cut off in traffic the other day by someone who had a "Live the Golden Rule" license plate (one of the many vanity plates one can get here in Arizona). Does that give me the right to cut that person off?
- Should I report that person and sue to have the plate rescinded?
- How should we respond to someone who has no regard for what the Golden Rule is all about?

- Is it more realistic to just accept that the one who has the gold rules?
- What does that say about who and what we are as a society?
- Would it ever be worth it to refrain from crossing the road?

Chapter Five

The Grasshopper

FROM THE WORLD OF my grandparents (may they rest in peace) I inherited the habit of giving nick-names to various people (usually the ones you might label as a "character") with whom I am engaged. There is one student who I refer to (to myself) as "The Grasshopper." I do so because, though it took me a few weeks to train him to do otherwise, more often than not, when he gets out of school and runs to the corner where I am crossing students, even as I am beginning to step into the street and raise the stop sign, he is already aiming for the middle of the intersection. I stop him (usually only get to slow him down) the best I can and ask (plead with!) him to wait until I give the signal to go ahead, as some drivers do not stop for anything. With The Grasshopper I have about an 80 percent success rate.

There is one little girl who often darts out as quickly as The Flash and runs behind me when I am just about to let the traffic continue. But she is so fast (and usually startles me!) that I have not had a chance to look at her to decide on a name.

The presence of these students, as well as the drivers who do not have the patience to ensure that all the students cross the street safely, makes me wonder: What is the rush? Where are these people going that they cannot wait the few seconds more that it will take to prevent any mishaps?

Why is everyone in such a rush? In terms of time, we are granted 24 hours each day. That breaks down into 1,440 minutes, or 86,400 seconds. We "spend time," "waste time," "save time," "lose time," and "make time." Sometimes we even "take the/our time," though from where and to where I am never really sure!

I remember when I was in sixth grade learning the value and length of time. I do not recall the exact circumstances that led up to the exercise, but it was obviously a lesson (punishment?) for something we had or had not done. The teacher had us all sit with our backs erect, our hands on our empty desks, and look straight ahead for one full minute, 60 seconds, by his count. It was the longest minute that I can ever remember. Though, more often than not, the passage of time often seems relative to what we may be doing or expecting, by itself, time is always the same. Each and every day has 24 hours, 1,440 minutes, 86,400 seconds (count them if you do not believe me!).

When we are young the days go quickly and the years are so long. With age, it seems that our days go on forever, while the years speed by, with particular moments (birthdays, anniversaries, deaths) sneaking up on us as if we were not looking.

What is it with time? Why do we rage/race against it as much as we cherish every moment? Perhaps Alice put it best. For, as she would have it (*Alice's Adventures in Wonderland*), "I know who I was when I got up this morning, but I think I must have been changed several times since then." Or, as she observes in another place, "I could tell you my adventures—beginning from this morning . . . but it's no use going back to yesterday, because I was a different person then."

What we do with the time that is allotted to us defines who we are. However, we are the ones who control that "doing."

Rabbi Menachem Mendel Schneerson (the late "Rebbe," the leader of worldwide Chabad) taught that, "This is the key to *time management*—to see the value of every moment." Far be it for me to contradict or argue with what he said. However, I would add one more thought: Seeing the value of every moment is significant if it leads us to value every moment that is ours. And that can be done with a little trick, something taught (and quoted far and wide) by (18th century) Rabbi Simcha Bunim of Parshischo (and no, I do not know how to pronounce that either!), who said that every person should have two slips of paper in his pocket. On one should be written: "The world was created for me." On the other should be written: "I am but dust and ashes." Our role, then, if we are to value the time that is ours, is to have the wisdom to know which slip of paper to read at the right time.

I wonder sometimes how intentional we are with the time that is ours. My tradition teaches that we are to live each day as if it is our last. That is hard to do and extremely humbling. It also contradicts what I said above about the need to live purposefully and with focus, which implies that we are (or at least can be) in control and the masters of our destiny. However, maybe that is one of the keys to living life fully and in synch with the time that is ours. It acknowledges that life can be messy, filled with confusion and contradictions. And yet, with a healthy appreciation for the way time can give us structure and help us to mark the flow of the seconds, minutes, hours, days, weeks, months, and years, we would find every one of the 86,400 seconds we are granted each day to be meaningful and significant.

I would like to know where it is The Grasshopper is off to when he leaves school and why he is in such a rush. I would also like the one I have referred to as The Flash, even if she will not slow down, to at least run in front of me instead of behind me, so I can manage the flow of traffic (automobile and human) at the corner a little better (ensure a higher degree of safety). For the time being, at least they seem to be living in their respective moments.

What about us? Are we just going through the motions? Or, is there a reason to the rhythm of our lives?

If you were approached and granted a year to do whatever you wanted, wherever you wanted to do it (with the guarantee that all would return to "normal" at its end), what would you choose? Would you look for a cruise ship that is circling the globe? Would you try to find a secluded beach with white sand and clear blue waters covering a colorful coral reef? Maybe you would want a cabin in the woods to explore a mountainous forest with your family and closest friends? Or, maybe you would want a gift card that would cover your trips to every mall in America, several times over!

Personally (and I never ask a question that I am not asking of myself), I would ask for the year to be "amortized" over the course of any number of years, which would, hopefully, ensure a long and productive life, as well as the opportunity to change my mind and learn from the moments that I had had. I am not sure what my first requests would be. However, I am pretty sure that they would revolve around having the time and opportunities to strengthen the relationships I have with the ones I love, and repair those I may have broken over time, as well as making sure that I do something(s) that makes the world a better place.

For many years I used to love to watch *Inside the Actors Studio* hosted by James Lipton. In front of an auditorium of film and media students, he would interview some of the biggest names/stars in the business. Along with the serious questions concerning the nature of their craft, he would also ask a string of questions that were a bit more human:

- What is your favorite word?

- What is your least favorite word?

- What turns you on?

- What turns you off?

- What sound or noise do you love?

- What sound or noise do you hate?

- What is your favorite curse word?

- What profession other than your own would you like to attempt?

The one question they all always got wrong was: "If heaven exists, what would you like to hear God say when you arrive at the pearly gates?" Most of the people described emotional moments wherein their humility, generosity, or wisdom, etc., was acknowledged, while the gates flew wide open. Me? I would want whoever is in charge to say something to the effect of "Oh, I am so sorry, we made a mistake, we will be sending you back down to earth to finish off a long life of health, wealth, and happiness . . . the elevator is right behind you! Do not rush, enjoy the time that is yours!"

And yet, as my tradition would have it, the best manner in which to "enjoy the time" is to ensure that when we depart from this world, we will be able to answer the following questions (paraphrased from the Babylonian Talmud Shabbat 31a):

- Were you honest in your business dealings? Did what and how you worked reflect the core values of our tradition?

- Did you set aside time to study and connect with that which is greater than all of us?

- Were you engaged in and with your family, investing in raising up a next generation?

- Were you focused on your tomorrows, on making the world a better place and those who inhabit it worthy of its presence?

- Did you engage with other people in exploring the depth of their wisdom, sharing experiences of life as it is lived?

- Did you believe . . . have faith in more than yourself . . . enable that faith to guide your steps from day to day?

I believe that most of us would (could, to some degree) say "Yes" to each of those questions and have an anecdote or two to prove it. However, does knowing that those are the questions that we will be asked at the end of our run impact on how we might (intentionally) spend our time?

- Why did the chicken cross the road?
  - How fast was she going?
  - What was the rush?
  - Why did she take so much time to make her mind up to take the first steps?

Change the word "chicken" (and "she") in this first series of questions to "you" and answer them.

- How are your answers the same/different?

- We often rush through life as if it is all ours and we are in complete control.
- Do you ever stop to ask yourself where you are really going?

- Review the questions I paraphrased from Shabbat 31a. At the end of your days, which of the questions would you have the hardest time answering?
- Why?

- How does "knowing that there is a test at the end" impact the way you are living your life?
- Does life always have to be so serious?
- Why can't we just enjoy it?
  - What do you enjoy doing the most?
  - What in your life is most meaningful to/for you?
    - Are your answers to the last two questions the same?

Chapter Six

Sagebrush Rolling Through the Open Air

So, IT IS SUMMER. I drove by the school to see how my corner was doing. I had fantasies of seeing a desolate plot of barren desert occupied only by a few balls of dry brown sagebrush drifting through what used to be a sometimes very busy intersection. How is that for an ego! If I was not there, then nothing else would (should) be either! The situation, however, was a bit different. All was as I had left it . . . trees, bushes, and plants all doing well (they have an automatic irrigation system). There were a few cars in the parking lot (administrators and teachers getting a jump on the beginning of school) and a stream of traffic (sparse though it was) obeying the speed limit and other street signs. Very humbling!

Or, was it?

Actually, maybe that is the way it is supposed to be. Maybe there was a lesson there that I needed to learn, especially if I was to understand why the chicken crossed the road!

Jewish tradition (Mishnah Chagigah 2:1) teaches, "One who contemplates four things, it would have been better had he not come into the world: what is above, what is beneath, what came before, and what comes after."

As the text is understood in its literal sense, it is telling us not to engage in speculative philosophy. It is impossible for us to truly understand everything that is in the heavens above (ask an astronomer and an honest one will tell you that we have more to learn than we will ever know), nor what is in the deepest depths of the earth, nor the secrets of what came before creation (or even the moment of), nor what will be in the future (which, though somewhat up to us, cannot be predicted). And, even if we could answer all of our questions regarding even one of these areas of concern, how would that knowledge help? No, as we are taught in Deuteronomy 29:28: *The secret things belong to the Lord our God; but that which is revealed belongs to us.*

On another level, I would suggest that the text is more concerned with what we should be doing rather than with what we should not. And what it is teaching us is the importance of being in the moment. I know that I wrote about this earlier, but it cannot be emphasized enough. When crossing the students my mind has to be focused on what is going on right then and there. There are certain cars/drivers that I recognize as "problematic," as well as some students. To shift my directions accordingly would be more than appropriate. However, if I am focused on what was, or what might be, then I would be distracted from the actuality of the moment that I am in.

So what? Who cares? What does any of this matter?

When I was engaged in congregational life and I had to meet with a family regarding a death and the planning for a funeral (and I probably officiated at over 2000 over the course of my career), I would always make it a point to tell the mourners that they should have only one expectation of/for themselves. And that was to have none! Their "task" was to not worry about what other people might be thinking, or how what they were or were not doing might look like to others. Their "task" was to stay in touch with themselves, to realize that they will be dealing with a myriad of conflicting emotions and the only way to grieve is to embrace those emotions and make them their own. That is to say, their objective was to be in that moment.

This is not to say that one can/should not have hopes, dreams, goals, and aspirations. It is, however, encouraging us to put those hopes, dreams, goals, and aspirations into perspective. I have always dreamed of being a philanthropist! Unless I begin to play and win the lottery, I do not think that that is going to happen. And yet, that does not mean that I cannot be charitable with what I do have and embrace each moment with which I am engaged with actions that will make the world a better place.

My corner may have been "empty" the day that I drove by. However, that was the way it was supposed to be. "Deal with it!" I told myself. In a little bit the corner will not be that empty anymore and I will have the same challenges that I had in the past. If I can make that past and what is yet to come as one, that will be a pretty good day . . . sagebrush or not!

So what? Who cares? What does any of this matter? My favorite questions! And, perhaps, one of the reasons I wrote this book.

Visit a local bookstore, or surf through the website of a company that sells books, and you will find a plethora of self-help books. I would venture to guess that in some stores it would be the largest section. And that is part of the problem with chickens crossing the road. They (and we!) get so caught up with what others tell us we are supposed to do that we lose sight of what it is that we want and/or need. As such, I want to suggest that this book should not be seen as a self-help book as much as an encouragement to begin to help ourselves to live life with everything we have.

Why, or how, the chicken crossed the road is not as important as what she did when she got there. We spend years in therapy wondering why or how to cross the roads that we are traveling, but do not take the time to focus on what we are doing when we do get across, at the given moment that we are in. If I have learned anything from my experience as a crossing guard it is to ensure that we need to do just that. We will get to where we need to be. Once we are there, it is ours to do it.

* * *

Our son and his family went out of town for vacation this week, so we have the honor of dog-sitting. I have written elsewhere of my relationship with Piper and how if she could talk one of us would have to go. Our 5 a.m. strolls around the neighborhood (before it gets too hot to go out) have not changed. This morning I realized that talking with her is very much time that I am also talking to myself. Maybe that is another example of what it means to confront the sagebrush (or lack thereof). I know that she gets mad at me when I do not let her chase after rabbits. But she loves me even more when I let her stop and sniff any bush, tree, plant, lamppost, or even barren piece of ground that she wants. We do not go that fast, but we always do seem to get to where we want and need to be. There is a lesson there, but I will leave it to you to figure it out.

Or not!

In the business world there is a trend, among some, of focusing on what are called "Moments that Matter." Essentially, these are moments that have an impact on an employee's experience. Maybe it is the special attention that is given to a new employee when they are brought on board: the attention given to helping the new employee manage the transition into the new position—helping them feel comfortable, or even the way someone says "Hello." Maybe it is the way a review is handled, ensuring that it is a moment of encouragement and growth. Maybe it is the way a manager finds out what really matters to an employee: what they would like to see their role and relationship become, what they would like to be valued for, and how that valuation is shared with them. What is important is understanding that the moments that an employee spends at work matter. The way we embrace that meaning will (or will not!) help that employee feel they are valued (understand the meaning their presence has in the bigger picture) as well.

In some ways, my walks with Piper helped me better understand the meaning of the moments that I have been granted in this life. There is a saying attributed to Mark Twain: "The two most important days in your life are the day you were born, and the day you find out why!" That saying is too profound to even begin to try to unpack. However, I would suggest that a response to the statement would be that it is, in part, our job to make the answer to the "why" count . . . to ensure that we make every moment a moment of meaning (or at least as many moments as we can).

Every moment can be "autotelic." (That is a great word that I heard the other day, which I had to look up! It means: something that contains its purpose within itself.). Every moment can be what we make of it . . . rather than we being made by it. Perhaps that is why are taught:

> *Yesterday is gone.*
> *Tomorrow is still a dream.*
> *But this moment is here . . . it is a gift . . . and that is why*
> *we call it "the present."*

* * *

So, let us get back to the sagebrush.

As I approached "my corner" that day there were so many things I could have been thinking about. Why was I so concerned with the fantasy? Probably, because like everyone else, rather than focusing on the moment . . . seeing it as "autotelic"—embracing it as part of what life is in and of itself . . . I let my ego prevail. Instead of being in that moment, I wanted that moment to be in me. Was it a Mark Twain "Why" moment? That I cannot confirm one way or the other. However, learning what I did from it, it sure comes close. That moment taught me a very important lesson. It taught me that moments do matter. And they matter most when we appreciate them for what they are.

- Why did the chicken cross the road?
  - Was she alone?
  - Did anyone notice when she was there and when she was gone?
  - What was she thinking about along the way?

Change the word "chicken" (and "she") in this first series of questions to "you" and answer them.

- How are your answers the same/different?

- What are your most heartfelt hopes, dreams, goals, and aspirations?
- Are there any dreams that you have had to let go of along the way?
- How did you accommodate those changes?

- Where do you go and with whom do you talk when you need an ear to help you hear what is going on in your life?

- What are your greatest expectations?
- What are your greatest disappointments?
- What are your greatest successes?

- What corner are you most concerned about crossing?
- What would help you to take those next steps?

Chapter Seven

They're Baaaaaaack!!!!!!!

I AM NOT A great fan of horror movies. Besides having enough drama in my life as it is, they are much too scary for me. And yet, when the commercial for the second *Poltergeist* movie came out showing a little girl picking up the ringing phone, turning, and saying (somewhat calmly) "They're baaaaaaack!!!" it made an impact on me. So much so that I almost went to see the movie (movies: first and second!). However, sanity prevailed, and I did not. The only way I will watch a horror movie is when I can see the ending first, so I know what to expect!

And yet, in just a week I will be back at my corner. With the first crossing I know I will softly chuckle to myself and say "They're baaaaaaack!" I will, hopefully, help them safely cross the street for their way back home and I will wonder: "And then what?" Now that they have crossed the road, what will they do next?

As I have said, why we cross any road as we do, move from moment to moment, can easily be explained. However, what we do when we arrive at that destination is what counts even more. So, what will these students do with all the good stuff they are learning inside those walls? For that matter, how do any of us process the moments that are ours so that we will one day look back and see that our lives were more than just long (I love that line, it is a play on the lyrics of one of the songs in *Pippin*. And, if you have not seen that play your life is not complete!).

I will admit, there are times (too many, in fact) when I am haunted by the moments that got away.

- The times that I fell short of what I could or should have done.
- The times when I am sorry for what I did do.
- The times that caused me to wonder just what time it was.

I wonder about those times regarding what could have been. However, those moments help me refocus on those that I do have.

So, there is a road in front of us. We are looking to get to the other side. Should we succeed, what will we do there? In many ways, the one enabling the crossing, and the one being crossed, should be considered as one and the same. With every step, we learn a little about ourselves and each other. Keeping this in mind could make the "And then what" that much more significant.

I am not trying to be overly profound here. I am suggesting that the meaning and significance of any, if not every, moment that is ours is very much influenced by the people we are with. I am not sure who said it first (a Google search provided multiple sources), but it is important to note that *life is a journey and not a guided tour*. To make the best of each step it is important to try to focus on what we are doing, and who we are doing it with.

Maybe the whole answer to this concern is to stay focused, even when we are meandering. Yes, they will be back. The question is, will we? Will we be ready to pick up where we left off? Even as we know that we are stepping into a raging river, which, though looking very much the same as where we left off, is not even close to being similar.

As I have sat and written these chapters I thought often about the title of the book. I worried that it sounded like the title of a book that might be found in an adult bookstore! I even played with changing it to something different. However, it really does describe my time on my corner, and how all those afternoons made me stop and think. Perhaps that is what we all should be doing once we cross the road and get baaaaaaack on track. Over the years, when meeting with people (congregants) who wanted to share concerns regarding how life was going for them, I always counseled them (within reason) not to regret their past . . . it made them who they are. Are we always proud of everything we have done? If someone says that they are, I would call them a liar. However, we can come baaaaaaack and start from where we left off. That is not a "do over." It is a next step down the path we call life.

According to Jewish law there is a particular manner in which one is supposed to put their shoes on (right, left, tie left, tie right). Some say the reason for the order is that the right side is the side of strength while the left is the side of devotion and attachment. Others say that it is because one side represents the attribute of mercy while the other is associated with judgment and discipline. Unpacking this any further would take us well beyond the scope of this "conversation," yet it speaks volumes regarding the importance of watching where we are going, and living with intentionality each day, from the very first moment that we get dressed, if we want life to have meaning and significance. I want to note that I used to ask groups that visited our synagogue for an introduction to Judaism class to take their shoes off, put them on, and then tell me the order in which they put their shoes back on. The majority of participants could not remember even though they had just completed the task. Case in point. Each and every day we have to be baaaaaaack.

In case you have not noticed, life is messy! We can make all sorts of plans that, even if we follow them, do not always work out the way they were supposed to. Even in the make-believe land of Hollywood, and for the celebrities of our popular culture, things do not work out as magically as they are supposed to. Pick up a copy of *People* magazine or watch the "culture" reports on the national news (especially the morning shows on the major networks), and you will see all too quickly how messy things are. The divorce rate in Hollywood, for those that actually do "tie the knot" (and I would venture to guess there is a high percentage of couples that do not), is over 50 percent (which is higher than the national average). Such star studded and overdone productions just do not make it in real life.

When we say we are "baaaaaaack," it is an indication that it is time to leave the land of make-believe behind and move on to what we believe we can (or at least will try our best to) make happen. Yes, life is messy. However, that is what makes it interesting/meaningful, and fun (at least some of the time, hopefully most of the time) as well. We cannot predict what is going to happen in life. We cannot control all the various forces that make up the road signs and determine the course of our path. However, more than just reacting to what happens to us, we can respond and make things happen through us. Crossing the road can be a metaphor for life, especially if we focus on what we are going to do once we are on the other side.

At this point, I want to emphasize that this conversation was never intended to be a systematic theology or psychology. It is mostly the rambling thoughts of someone who may have had a little too much time on their hands (please do not tell my school, they may dock me!). And at times it sounds repetitive. However, the thinking is what enabled me to cross the roads that I have had to over the past year(s), and I share them hoping that you might find some insight for your journey as well.

Every day that is ours gives us a chance to start all over again. Not "do over," but, rather, start over, even/especially if that means picking up where we left off the day before. I hope that as you put one foot in front of the other and cross the road to get to wherever it is that you are going, like all the chickens, you will know what it is that you want to accomplish on the other side . . . and do it well.

- Why did the chicken cross the road?
  - How many times has she been in this situation?
  - Why does she seem to keep coming back and starting all over again?
  - What is she trying to accomplish?
  - What will it take for her to get there?

Change the word "chicken" (and "she") in this first series of questions to "you" and answer them.

- How are your answers the same/different?

- What are some of the moments in your life that you regret?
- How have they made you into the person that you are?
- How can you take whatever negative energy that may persist and allow it to enable you to be more positive about yourself?

- If you had any advice to give to the "chickens" that you are helping to cross the road, what would it be?
- What would you have liked someone to have told you?

- What is your next step going to look like?

Chapter Eight

She Loves Me Not? She Loves Me!

THE FIRST COUPLE DAYS of school were "a hoot"! The line of cars in the pick-up lanes went completely around the school and stayed that way for 20 minutes! Some kids walk, some get picked up. However, I have never seen such unmitigated attention to pick-up time in my (short though it may be) career. Why such attention to the personal pick-up? Why can't the students just go home? It may have something to do with that four-letter word: L-O-V-E. Or, maybe it was . . . ?

So, what is love? In the stream of parenting, it is often translated into obligation and/or responsibility. We attend to our children because that is what we are supposed to do. Sometimes it even comes naturally, as something we want to do. However, that does not answer the question.

When talking or thinking about love, the first thing that comes to mind is a song/scene from *Fiddler on the Roof*. Tevye asks Golde if she loves him. She replies:

> *Do I love you?*
> *For twenty-five years I've washed your clothes*
> *Cooked your meals, cleaned your house*
> *Given you children, milked the cow*
> *After twenty-five years, why talk about love right now?*

When Tevye asks again, she responds:

SHE LOVES ME NOT? SHE LOVES ME!

Do I love him?
For twenty-five years I've lived with him
Fought him, starved with him
Twenty-five years my bed is his
If that's not love, what is?

Which is to say, love is defined not by words, but by deeds. Sitting in a hot car in a school pick-up line perhaps?

And yet, I am also reminded of a story: The funeral was very small: the rabbi, the woman's husband and children, and just a few of their closest friends. The woman had not been sick; her death came unexpectedly. There really were no words to say. The rabbi's eulogy was short and to the point: "We know why we are here. There really are no words which will make this moment easier. With all of our private memories bursting within the confines of our hearts, let us ensure that she is given the tribute that she deserves . . . that her memory will remain among us as a living and a loving benediction." The casket was lowered and everyone except the husband returned to their cars. The husband just stood by the side of the grave staring at the casket, murmuring: "I loved her . . . I loved her." The rabbi walked up next to the man and put his arm around his shoulders and lightly hugged him. The man just kept murmuring: "I loved her . . . I loved her." The rabbi, who knew the family well, tried to comfort the man by reminding him of everything he had done for the woman in life, how attentive he had been, how happy his wife had been, and how they had grown such a beautiful family. The man, however, just kept murmuring: "I loved her . . . I loved her." The rabbi and the man stood next to each other in silence until the man finally said, "I loved her, rabbi. And one time I almost told her."

The first time (actually, one and only time) I used that story, the memorial service, which was quiet already, became even more still than one could imagine. I had to look carefully to see if people were still breathing. It obviously struck a nerve.

There are some who use the word love indiscriminately and repetitively. These are the people who might say: "Oh, chicken for dinner? I love chicken!" To whom I would respond, if you really love chicken(s) you would not eat them! Others are much more reserved. One could wonder if the word "L-O-V-E" is even in their vocabulary. And yet, they are demonstrably invested in being there with and for people, especially those who are their significant others.

Love is a relative term. There are different types of love (e.g.: platonic, familial, romantic, etc.), and different degrees among each of those. However, I am beginning to believe that one of the most important variations is the one that brings parents to the pick-up lanes. Though there is probably a more accepted term for it, I am going to describe this love as "parental love." This is the type of love that inspires someone to hold on to an other tightly in order to let them go.

It is an irony of parenting that, at least in this modern age, our purpose is to raise our children so that they can go out on their own. Not so long ago, children were a factor in the economic stability of a family: the more children, the more one could tend to the farm or even the emerging business. Now the factors involved with the decision to have children are very different. They might be social, religious, or even biological. I remember a woman coming to me and asking if she should have more children, or was it just her womb speaking. I told her that I would be more than willing to discuss her concern from a religious perspective. However, I also suggested that it was a conversation that she should better have with her husband. In the end, they stopped with the two children they already had.

I would suggest that one of the best images for understanding the idea of parental love is the manner in which a butterfly emerges from its chrysalis. So, a story:

> Once a little boy found a chrysalis that had fallen from a tree. He showed it to his mother who explained what it was, and how it protected a once-thriving caterpillar while it began its transformation into a butterfly. The boy grew very excited and took the chrysalis up to his room where he protected it and watched it for hours on end, day after day after day. Eventually he saw the chrysalis

begin to move and a hole begin to appear at one of its ends. He watched the butterfly begin to emerge with fascination—how it struggled with the small space it had to contend with. However, suddenly the butterfly stopped. It seemed to have given up the struggle to get out of the chrysalis. The boy had become attached to the butterfly and did not want to see it (what he believed was) suffering. He got out a small pair of scissors and enlarged the hole so the butterfly was able to free itself from the confines of the chrysalis. There was one problem. Because the butterfly had not endured the entire struggle/process and squeezed excess fluid out of its wings, etc. it was unable to fully transform. Instead of drying off and flying away, the butterfly was only able to drag itself across the ground, weighted down by its unusable wings.

And so it is with our children.

Parental love can be stifling, so overprotective and intrusive/invasive, that the child never has an opportunity to develop the skills it needs to live life fully. Helicopter parents, as challenging as they were, have transformed into "dirigibles"! They hover and never go away. Should the child get a skinned knee the parents are ready to file a police report: negligence, assault, whatever might fit the crime.

When I was working full-time, I used to tape cartoons or pictures on the outside of my office door. In the center of the door, however, was an opinion piece from *Newsweek* magazine. The piece was entitled: "We Protect Kids From Everything But Fear," which is why I put it up. It caught my attention because it is so often true. There are some who are so concerned with the well-being of their children that they never let them wriggle out of their chrysalis . . . develop the strength and fortitude to make the kind of decisions that will enable them to live happy and healthy lives. So much so that one of the most disturbing trends that I see among post-high school young adults is a certain degree of angst regarding the future. They have no idea of what they want out of life or are so driven by what their parents taught them they were supposed to be doing that they do not know what life is to begin with.

Parental love is meant to be liberating. It is meant to inspire us to hold on so tightly that we can let go with confidence. It is easy to talk about. It is hard to accomplish. However, it is a task which, when embraced well, can lead to amazing things. Perfect we will never be. But engaged and intentional we can always be.

In fact, parental love is very similar to serving as a crossing guard. The purpose is to help our children get to a place where they will be able to take their next steps in the direction that they want or need to go. Are we left behind? In some ways, yes. But that is the joy: watching them go off on their own.

Waiting in a pick-up lane on a hot summer day can be a chore. However, if it leads (metaphorically speaking) to helping a child transition from one side of the road to the other, then the effort is more than worth it.

* * *

An aside: In the Jewish tradition, when a child reaches majority status (i.e. is to be considered an adult), the parents recite a special prayer praising God for releasing them from the responsibility of their (the child's) behavior. What is interesting to me is that such transition is said to happen when the child reaches early adolescence. For a boy, at 13, just as the hormones begin to pump and the process of individuation begins to emerge as a motivating force (urge?!) in that child's path toward self-realization. Though I often joke that the rabbis instituted that practice somewhat "tongue in cheek," they knew that hormonally challenged teenagers and custodial parents do not always share the same concerns (how is that for being politically correct?!), who were they kidding? They knew that giving parents an out for the next decade or so of what are (for so many) tumultuous years at best would ensure that all could survive. However, it also captures the essence of parental love: holding on so tight that you can let go.

Saying that prayer, and meaning it, is very scary. It demands a great deal of trust in ourselves (that we did what we were supposed to for those first 13 years), in our child (that they will actually use the common sense with which they were endowed for good), and in our world as a whole (that there will be good cause and support for them to do/find the good in themselves without the distractions that can/would lead them astray). However, maybe Golde did have it right . . . love is what we do (or, in this case, did) and it is up to our children to provide the commentary through the manner in which they will live their lives. To love is to remember that though we cannot always control, we have an obligation to influence as best we can . . . whether they like it or not . . . and hope for the day when we can look at them and say (as I love to remind my son when his children are being giving him a hard time, similar to what he did to us): Karma is a B****! We need to love them as much as we do so we can let go.

- Why did the chicken wait so long to cross the road?
  - How many times has she been in this situation?
  - Is it a matter of patience or perseverance?
  - What is she trying to accomplish?
  - What will it take for her to get moving again?

Change the word "chicken" (and "she") in this first series of questions to "you" and answer them.

- How are your answers the same/different?

- What are some of the moments in your life that were worth waiting for?
- How have they made you into the person you are?
- How can you take whatever negative energy that may persist and allow it to enable you to be more positive about yourself?

- If you had any advice to give to the "chickens" that are waiting to cross the road, what would it be?
- What would you have liked someone to have told you?

- What is your next stop going to look like?

- Where is your love directed the most?
- Do you express or exhibit your love?
  - Which is more important to do?
  - How do you do it?
- Do you expect anything in return?
- How do we ensure that those we love know that we do . . . even in their most difficult times?

- In what ways are you holding on as tightly as you can in order to let them go?

Chapter Nine

It Takes a What?

THOUGH MY CAR REGISTERED the temperature at 111 degrees, the Weather Channel said it only got up to 109. It was obviously a cool day!

Beginning this year, I have had an hour or so added to my shift so I can help with some of the busy work in, especially, the office. Today I filed some kind of assessment form results for the fourth, fifth, and sixth graders. Except for the names, I was careful not to look at the forms in detail. The information is confidential. However, I had a field day with the names. I felt like I was working at the United Nations. Even if the families were second-generation and fairly Americanized, their roots (at least if the names were of any indication) went around the world. And yet, here we were, one school, one community, with a common purpose and a common intent to make this the best school it could be.

Did I hear someone say: "It takes a village"? Well, that may be true in American politics. But today, at the school where I work, it took a popsicle!

109? 111? In truth, what is the difference? I am from upstate New York, where anything over 60 is considered warm. So, while I am at my corner, I make sure I get in the shade when I can, and drink water whether I want it or not. Today, in the middle of one of the busiest crossings, one of the parents reached out and said, "Here, have a popsicle!" I know I tried to say, "Thank you!" It came as a complete surprise. So much so that I was a little taken aback, and unable to really focus on the moment. Besides, there was a mess of kids that I had to get across the street. The first opportunity I had I opened the popsicle up and began to eat it (if I had not it would have been a puddle in my pocket before I knew it). Obviously, a few of the kids asked where they could get one. However, most of the parents just smiled and nodded as if to say, "Good for you!"

Over the course of the crossings during the past few days, many of the parents have made comments about how hot it is and asked if I was OK, often adding their suggestions regarding how I could stay cool. And the popsicle put it all in perspective.

What is a village? What is a community? What does it take to come together as one? In Hebrew, a word that is often used for what we would call a community is "*edah.*" The root of that word is "*eid,*" which means "witness." This suggests that what makes a group of disparate individuals into something more is when they come together and bear witness to and for each other, validating the importance of each and every individual to and for and with every other.

I believe that it is pretty much presumed that there is a mandate to educate our children. And, there are, today, a number of different options through which to fulfill that mandate: public schools, private schools, parochial schools, charter schools, home-schooling, etc. Where we send our children is to some degree a matter of choice. We look for a school that reflects our sense of mission, vision, and values. That is, we want an educational environment that, in form and function, will help us develop our children's characters to become positive and contributing members of our community. It is as if the school itself is a crossing guard of sorts, helping the students to transition from one stage in their lives to the next. And giving them the skills to continue to grow throughout their lives. In a different lifetime, I used to tell our teachers (and the counselors at a summer camp I worked at for 10 years), "Your students/campers may not remember everything you say to them. However, they will remember how you said it." As for the teacher or counselor, so for the school as a whole.

No educational environment is or will be perfect. To succeed there must be a certain degree of compromise regarding specific paths that are taken. However, to choose one particular school over another is a statement regarding one's desire to make that investment.

Yes, sometimes a popsicle is just a popsicle (I got another one today! Two in a row!). However, why such gifts are extended is an outcome of what it means to be "a village" . . .or, better, an *edah*

Obviously, this school is doing something right!

- You see a chicken in the process of crossing the road.
  - What would you give that chicken to help her?
  - What do you think the chicken would like to be given?

Change the subject in this first series of questions to you/yourself and answer them.

- How are your answers the same/different?

- What are your mission, vision, and values?
- How are they reflected through the way you are living your life?
- How are you passing them on to your children?

- Amid this journey we call life, what are the different communities of which you are a part?
- How are they helping you with your "crossings"?

Afterword

GOOGLE "WHY DID THE chicken cross the road?" and you will receive: about 116,000,000 results (in 0.33 seconds). Granted, some of the results might be a bit repetitive. However, it is obvious that it is a question of interest. Is it a critical conundrum? In most cases probably not. It is usually asked as more of a joke than anything else. So why did I ask it (so to speak)? What is/was the concern?

As I mentioned, my time on my corner lends me abundant opportunities to just think. Though this text was in no way meant to be a systematic "psychology" or "theology," still, the question of the chicken crossing the road enabled me to find a certain structure to my thoughts. I have always been fascinated with the impact of intention(ality) on the manner in which we are living our lives. And how anyone might cross a road as they do is a perfect example of where the two concerns intersect.

Things have started to calm down on my corner. It seems that the parents are starting to get their rhythm down. And as my crossers go, I am beginning to think that time has caused the "anonymity" to begin to dissipate. Very few have stopped to ask my name. However, there seem to be many more smiles and "Thank You's" than last year. Perhaps familiarity breeds content!

There are a myriad of thoughts that engage me as I stand at my corner. It may be the heat! However, I believe (lest I get a head ache) that it is best to stop here. The truth of the matter is that no matter how many people might cross at my corner, as it was for the chicken, so it is probably for most of us . . .

Why did the chicken cross the road?
To get to the other side!

If we can do at least that, then we can also say that life is good!

* * *

The first rough draft of this manuscript was finished during the first month of school (August). I showed what I had to the principal and administrator to ensure (though I tried to leave the "characters" anonymous) that there would be nothing of concern or embarrassment. However, I decided to put it down until after the Jewish Holy Days before beginning the editing and polishing process. That delay, for a number of reasons, lasted until Hanukkah, which ended up being a good thing.

A story: When we were in Tucson my wife asked me to accompany her to her school's "Holiday Party." I use the quotes because it was anything but. It was a Christmas party with no concern for those who might not celebrate that holiday and find themselves marginalized at that time of the year (and in this situation, I believe it was with intent). In any event, I said I would go. However, because it was a night of Hanukkah, I insisted on wearing my menorah hat (a stuffed menorah that cannot be missed). My wife was not excited about that idea, but it was the cost of having me accompany her. I told her that, given the neighborhood in which the school was situated, there had to be Jewish kids/families. I wanted to show my solidarity and support. For the most part, the hat was received cheerfully. Many people (except the principal) said "Happy Hanukkah" and smiled. At one point my wife had to go to the office to pick something up. As we went into the hall, I told her about the reaction I was getting. After a few steps, we walked by two fifth- or sixth-grade girls sitting in the hall by themselves talking. I did not think it was an unusual scene until they looked up at me, saw the hat, and said, "Thank you." Whatever embarrassment I may have caused to myself or others was redeemed by that "Thank you."

I am thoroughly convinced that if most Jews knew what Hanukkah was all about, they would not celebrate it! It has become for all too many a "Jewish Christmas," an alternative celebration so that our children (we!) do not feel left out of the season. As an aside, I remember when our kids were in elementary school being asked to come into the class to discuss Hanukkah. Though I felt very uncomfortable doing so, given my role in the community and the concerns regarding religion in the schools, that year I had a justifiable excuse. Because of the way the Jewish calendar falls, Hanukkah was already over. The teacher was beside herself: "Well I haven't covered it yet so we will just have to celebrate it anyway."

In truth, Hanukkah is much more than a Jewish Christmas, or a celebrate-on-demand social experience. The story begins in ancient Israel when the Greeks decided that the Jews had to go, one way or another. Many had already assimilated and/or given up any desire to be identified as Jews, but enough were left to be of concern. So, emissaries were sent out to "encourage" the Jews to convert. When one such emissary entered the village of Modi'in and began pressuring the people to give up the foundation of who and what they were, he was met with resistance. Then one person decided to publicly respond in an attempt to mollify the emissary. Instead of making peace with the emissary, he ignited a war among the Jews. The revolt began with the killing of that Jew who sought to calm things down. Hanukkah is not a celebration of religious freedom, it is a statement regarding the fight for religious freedom, that the Jews have just as much right to live as the distinct people that we are as anyone else. Hanukkah is the anti-assimilation effort that has kept us alive for centuries. It is ironic that it falls as it does in seeming conjunction with Christmas, but that is what makes it the powerful moment that it is.

And so, as I approached my duties in the school office as well as on my corner, for these nights of Hanukkah I have been wearing my menorah hat. I have to say, I know I lived in a bubble, but I did not expect the focus on Christmas to be as intense as it is at "my" school. I have seen innumerable Christmas trees on teachers' desks and have yet to see even one menorah. The school as an institution has tried to walk a balance beam focusing on the holiday spirit. But I could not help but wonder what the Jewish kids (and there are many) were feeling. So, with my hat on I have roamed the halls, entered classrooms, and tended to my corner. I cannot count the number of smiles I have received from the students, and the nods, as if to say, "Thank you." "I like your hat" has become code for more than one student as a statement of their moment of empowerment. And the number of cars that have stopped to give me thumbs up, or to thank me for wearing the hat, has been most encouraging for me. I wore the hat with a little trepidation, not knowing what the school would say. However, no one said much more than "nice hat." This afternoon I spoke with the principal and told her the story of what happened in Tucson and the similar response that I seemed to be getting here. I also thanked her for suffering through the embarrassment I may be causing to the school by standing out in front with the hat. In the end, however, these moments helped me bring this whole confession together, and to a conclusion.

There is one parent who always made it a point to wave and smile when he came to pick up his child and when he left. The first day that I wore the menorah hat, I could see his face and body language change considerably. He has stopped saying hello and/ or acknowledging my presence in any way. In fact, he makes it a point to stay on the other side of the street and crosses on his own, outside of the crosswalk. Instead of any kind of greeting, I get what I would consider "dirty looks"(when compared to how I used to be greeted). If the opportunity ever arises, I will ask what happened to change his manner as it has. I do not know what troubles him. But I do know that he has impacted on my Hanukkah experience. I am not sure that that hat will ever leave my head again. Maybe that is the point in the first place: If you do not stand for something, you will fall for any/everything. That does not leave much room for any kind of purposeful forward motion!

* * *

What does it take to get up, get going, and, at least figuratively, cross the road?

First, one needs to know where they are coming from, who they are, and what they stand for.

Second, one needs to know where they want to go. The path taken and the final destination may change with time. However, there is only one way to get "there" and that is take the first and second and third steps.

If we are not true to ourselves why should anyone else be?

Every day provides us with the opportunity for a new adventure. If my contemplative confession leads me to any kind of conclusion, it is that if we want to cross the road (live our lives with meaning and significance!), we had better do it because no one is going to do it for us.

You are the chicken!

You find yourself in the middle of the street. Don't worry, there is no traffic!

- Look back at all the places from which you came, what do you see? What defined you at the many different places in your life"
- Look at where you are right now. What do you see? Where would you like to be 1, 3, 5, 10 years from now? What would you like to look back on as your greatest accomplishment(s)?
- Looking backwards and forward at the same time, what is it going to take for you to get where you want to go?
- What will it take you to cross the street?

With all this said, how can I continue on this journey called life with a smile . . . and get rid of this headache that has been plaguing me because of all the questions ?!?!?!

Also by Robert J. Eisen

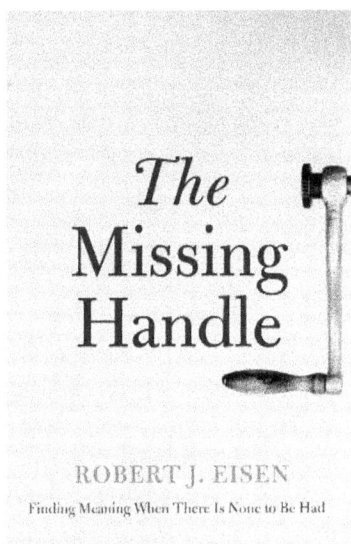

The Missing Handle

ROBERT J. EISEN
Finding Meaning When There Is None to Be Had

Ricky died. What do we do now?

This book is based on the journal kept by the author in response to the death of his 28-year-old son. The text offers a diary of the experience as well as how the mourning was processed from a Jewish perspective. It offers questions and counsel for anyone who has (and, who has not?) experienced the death of a loved one. It looks at what happens when life is experienced up close and personal, forcing us to ask questions we always thought belonged to someone else. What is it like when you look in a mirror and wonder how what you have been saying to people for so many years is yours to hear as well? It approaches the process of mourning from a personal perspective, offering reactions and responses that most mourners experience but rarely embrace (which is necessary for the healing process).

"Rabbi Eisen has marshalled a thousand generations of wisdom together with his and his family's very personal encounter with tragedy to craft a compelling reflection on sorrow, grief, and, above all, faith.

Only people of profound faith can confess to periods of doubt and only rationalists with heart will see meaning and purpose where others see only coincidence and happenstance. If you have ever been lost in the shadowed Valley of Death, Rabbi Eisen's experience will shine some light on those shadows."

—Perry Raphael Rank, rabbi emeritus, Midway Jewish Center

"Rabbi Eisen has given us all a gift of allowing himself to be fully human and vulnerable in offering authentic reflection on living before, during, and after the death of his son Ricky. He invites us to allow doubt as our first step towards faith, normalizing the wrestling process and celebrating multiple competing messy feelings. This invitation allows us to witness all the parts of ourselves, welcome them all in, and work towards living in line with our values while listening to our hearts.

—Autumn Wiley-Hill, clinical psychologist

"I have been honored to be a friend of Rabbi Eisen for many years. While we have served in different faith traditions, we have sought to respect, understand, and learn from each other. This book speaks to people of all faiths who grieve, and we all need help to grieve well. I hope you'll read this with eyes of faith to discover powerful truths that will not only help you to mourn, but find life through the grieving."

—Glen Elliott, campus pastor, Pantano Christian Church

AVAILABLE THROUGH

Amazon
Barnes & Noble
Wipf & Stock